About the Author

Born in 1950s England, the Author grew up in a South Manchester Council Estate and was raised within a family of seven. This no-nonsense book will be a valuable source of information to all those readers who endeavour to read it. Written from the heart, the author conveys a wealth of knowledge and experience from his own lifetime encounters. Written by the working class for the working class – and anybody else who is on this level – *A Shoestring and a Prayer* offers all readers the chance to learn how to cope the best way possible in these difficult times that lie ahead. Honest facts and eminent truths from a straight-talking individual who lives on the same level and walks the same streets. A must read for anyone in hard times.

# A Shoestring and a Prayer

Howard Hoyle

A Shoestring and a Prayer

Vanguard Press

VANGUARD PAPERBACK

© Copyright 2025
Howard Hoyle

The right of Howard Hoyle to be identified as author of this work has been asserted by him in accordance with the Copyright, Designs and Patents Act 1988.

All Rights Reserved

No reproduction, copy or transmission of this publication
may be made without written permission.
No paragraph of this publication may be reproduced,
copied or transmitted save with the written permission of the publisher, or in accordance with the provisions
of the Copyright Act 1956 (as amended).

Any person who commits any unauthorised act in relation to this publication may be liable to criminal prosecution and civil claims for damages.

A CIP catalogue record for this title is available from the British Library.

ISBN 978-1-83794-612-9

*Vanguard Press is an imprint of
Pegasus Elliot Mackenzie Publishers Ltd.*
www.pegasuspublishers.com

First Published in 2025

**Vanguard Press
Sheraton House Castle Park
Cambridge England**

Printed & Bound in Great Britain

Dedication

This book is dedicated to my nephew,
Christian,
who was taken too early.
R.I.P.
1975–2023

Acknowledgements

*I see your face from Afar,
Distant on that bright shining star,
All things we must learn and find Anew,
Bright one, what shall we do. H.*

Preface

This book is about how to cope with the minimum income in times of crisis. I do very much hope that it will help all those people who take the time and trouble to read this book.

Introduction

This is not a book aimed at any professional economist, but rather any individual person who has fallen into hard times, regardless of creed, colour, race or religion.

The purpose of this book is to help people understand how to succeed and survive in times of crisis. How to cope when money's tight, how to economise and cut down costs, how to manage without those items you really don't need any more, how to eke out things, waste nothing, use up the leftovers, and make do to make ends meet. And hopefully you all go to bed with some food in your stomach and not just fresh air.

Sounds like fun, not really, but being hard up never is. I know myself from personal experiences. This is not a cookery book but will contain some frugal recipes later on.

Due to this cost of living crisis we all now are going through, and prices going through the roof as we speak. This year, 2023, will be remembered by all, especially for our unreliable English summer. Do not, however, lose hope; you will survive; there is light at the end of the tunnel. You have to learn to take it one day at a time. And you will get through this day. Tomorrow is another day. Tackle this when you wake up tomorrow, but for now concentrate on today. I do hope that this book will help; if it only helps one person to succeed, then all the efforts will not have been in vain.

Street names you may have heard for being short of money:

Hard up, skint, peppermint, brassic lint, empty pockets, pockets full of sand, skid row, bankrupt, hard times, on your upper's, on your knees, and on your arse.

You may well have heard each and all of these phrases, and more besides, all of the ones mentioned above, as you well know, mean the same thing: no money. I've often thought when times were rough in the past, what a lovely world it would be if we didn't use money. Maybe in the next life, ahh?

Chapter One
Realisation

One only has to remember and look back on your past experiences in life once you are past twenty-five to thirty plus to realise what goes around, comes around. It may seem to some to be an old wives tale, but I think there is some truth in the phrase.

In life, good times and bad can come and go like the wind. Only to return again some years later. Life teaches you many things; the grass is always greener on the other side of the fence. Not always true. Having plenty of money makes you happy. Again, not always true. Just take a look at how many super stars, both rich and wealthy people, die early in their lives: Michael Jackson, Whitney Houston, and George Michael, to name but three. They seem to the laymen to have everything in their lives that you could possibly want, fame, fortune, etc., but somewhere within there's a big void. What exactly is it that is missing?

I'm not a religious person; the only time I go to church is for weddings, christenings, and funeral services, but I do believe that there is a God up there, somewhere.

Mental and spiritual attitude is the way to go.

You don't have to look back far into history to observe our forefathers, WW2, as they all toiled away into the dark shadows of the war, to observe their resilience, resourcefulness, courage, and just pure grit, of how they all hung on to their lives in order to survive. This is mental spirit and attitude. This is what you need to function and survive.

Big question: where does it come from?

It comes from within yourself; nobody else just you, you are your best and only friend you can rely on. Friends and family may well be there, but not always, but you are always there, within yourself, and that's where your strength comes from.

Accepting the truth and reality that you are now going into a dark period, that things are going to get tough, that you and fate are coming to blows, and that your financial situation and status are not as good as they once were. Do not despair; in time things will improve.

It takes a while, it takes work, it takes guts, but stick to your guns, and you will pull through, and one day you'll look back at all of this, and you'll wonder what all the fuss was about.

The first problem has now been solved, that is, you have realised you do have a problem.

Being broke is not the end of the world, although some would think so.

The last thing you need is to think along those lines; that is, the end of the road is just around the corner. That your world has fallen apart, your independence has ceased to exist, and your dignity has come to an abrupt end.

Poverty can be a dignity buster; if you let it be so, try to keep your mind off feeling down; do not let your emotions sink into an all-time low; rather, think about how resilient you are, and how you will solve this problem, and remember how bulletproof you can be in this time of crisis.

Never let it be said that the human mind is not a resourceful and resilient piece of equipment. When pushed, it's better than a computer. And it appears that the more it's pushed and tested, the better its performance.

I am no psychiatrist or psychotherapist. I'm just an ordinary Joe in the street, but past experience has taught me well, and the phrase, never say die, comes to mind.

Tough times require tough people.

So from this moment on, think like one, act like one, because you are one. Or you will very soon become one. Remember bulletproof. And you will survive.

Chapter Two
Acceptance

It is not every day you encounter this type of hardship; thank goodness. It does, I suppose, depend upon your class and your luck. Here in the U.K. there are still class distinctions: the upper classes, middle classes, and lower classes. Today, however, there is nowhere near as much as there was in the nineteenth century.

The lower-working-class person is more likely to experience times like these than those people in the middle and upper classes. They will always have a reserve to fall back on in hard times. This I encourage you yourselves to adopt when you get yourself off these difficulties. Although it may seem now to be an impossible astronomical sum of just £200 or $200 in reserve is recommended and the place to be. Then you will always have some security, and you yourselves will not be vulnerable if these times come back one big full circle to bite you in the arse. Hopefully not. Just that small sum can be the difference between food in your belly or not. Keeping your morale up, especially if you have children. Kids are very adaptable, and they can tolerate and withstand many different challenges and situations, but not hunger. I know this from raising my own son; he could withstand cold, could withstand poverty, and doing without the things that kids want, at least for a while. However, he would draw the line at being hungry. I made sure that he never went to bed with an empty stomach.

I remember watching a young lady on TV who was expecting her daughter home from school that afternoon. And all she had in her purse was 20p, and she had no food for dinner that day. My heart went out to her; you can't do much with 20p. To all our U.S.A. readers, that's about a quarter 25c. It is, no doubt, a pitiful place to be.

There are many reasons why we can find ourselves in these circumstances.

Divorce, redundancy, on benefits or welfare – these circumstances may well be of your own making. They may not be, but all that now seems irrelevant.

All your main concerns are focused on what is best for your future plans, and like that young lady, what is for tonight's dinner?

There is a world of difference in having two options. Then there is only having two chances. That is, a dog's chance, and no chance.

Option one will be food; option two could be heating; that was the way I went, because you can always wrap up and put on another layer to keep warm, but food is more important. To heat or eat, that is the question. My opinion is that there is no contest; food is first and foremost above everything else. If you have children, you can all cuddle up on the couch and giggle at the situation, watching TV. Morale will stay high, huddled up together under the quilt. This will only happen, however, if you all have some food in your bellies.

It does not need to be anything elaborate; anything will do, humble types of food.

It doesn't matter what, but there must be something, or else you will have problems.

You will also soon realise that the child will be fussy and choosy about what they eat. And that they won't eat; all goes out of the window.

They won't eat this; they won't eat that; it soon stops when they realise that there is nothing else.

Two chances, this food or nothing, take your pick; this is a good thing for the parents.

It means less problems for Mum and Dad, and it's a good education for the children because they learn to appreciate, accept, and enjoy their food. All be it a hard education.

Keep them happy if you can, then there'll be no revolt. It will not be easy for the parents, like trying to plait fog or sawdust on this very limited budget.

Do not worry or despair; things will pan out OK. But remember, swallow your pride, and always remember that life is just life, no matter where you live, and this is a good lesson for all of us.

Chapter Three
Solutions

The phrase tighten your belt all of us have heard sometimes in our lives. You can tighten it once, tighten it twice, then tighten it once again, but there comes a time when you can't tighten it any more. If you do, you will probably faint or pass out. The plain fact is, as every adult knows in these circumstances, is the absolute necessity to do just that. Tighten up, cut back, cut down, and economise on everything. This is the old-fashioned, old-school way. This is just how our forefathers did it – when the war was on, when the Great Depression struck, or when the recessions bite deep. We all have to economically let go of many different things that we normally take for granted. The point now is that things are not normal.

Let us shortly take a close look at the things we can economise on. The things we can do without, the things that we don't need. First though, let us take a look at the things we can NOT do without.

Very obviously, the first thing is the home, house, apartment or whatever your accommodation is. This is the top priority – to keep the roof over your head.

Any default on your mortgage or missing payments on your rent can and will cause major problems ahead.

You must at the first opportunity discuss your situation and circumstances with your lender, A.S.A.P. Do not bury your head in the sand like an ostrich. Then live in hope that your problems will disappear, because they won't. Face the situation square on and deal with the problem quickly. A good lender will or should bend over backwards to help the situation; it's in their interest to do just that; you are their business, and they do not want to lose you.

Once you have remedied this problem, you can relax, but only a little. The most important thing is the fact that your lender knows the situation and both of you are dealing with the problem.

Utilities/bills, gas and electricity, water and council tax.

Each and every one of these should also be contacted, and solutions hopefully brought into action. I say hopefully, because experience has taught me that some of these companies are harder to deal with than your lender.

Tell them that you want to switch over to a different tariff; if possible, that is the lowest possible payment that they can offer you. Remember the company that is hard to deal with. And in the future, you can switch to another company.

Food, obviously, this goes without saying; per annum, this is a serious bill. You can economise drastically in many areas; learning to cook properly and cheaply is without doubt one of the best ways to improve your meals and reduce your bill. If you can't cook, then learn how to. More on this later.

Once you have these things under control, then you'll have a little breathing space.

The end game here is to cut yourself some slack and create yourselves some time.

Remember though that it won't last forever; this is a temporary solution, and one that, in time, hopefully you will resolve.

The only way to change and rectify this situation fast is to get a job, any job.

Every man or woman has to earn a living to bring home the bacon.

There are many reasons why someone sometimes cannot work, i.e., illness, children.

The hours don't suit because they clash with the kids pick-up times from school.

There are many and varied reasons that hold you back, but the sooner you get working, the sooner things will return to normal. Shoestring survival is hard to cope with, and a job lifts the weight off your shoulders overnight. The knowledge that your monthly pay cheque is coming in at the end of the month. This is sweet music to you and your family. Also, getting up for work each morning gives you a sense of purpose. It gives you good vibes; it's therapeutic, so go for it, people. Good luck!

And remember, when you're this low, the only way you can go is up.

We now face the uncomfortable choice of cutbacks. The choice of what you cut back on is, of course, your own personal preference. The fact is, though, the more items you cut back on, the better. This is the brutal reality that you now face. You have to take steps and make decisions that will make a difference to your outgoings.

The more skint you are, the more you need to reduce costs.

Electricity items, electric appliances such as kettles and toasters, are very expensive to run. Put these in the cupboard and use a stove top kettle. Make your coffee, tea and toast with gas. It is four times cheaper. Of course this is only possible if you have gas; if you are all electric, then use the stove and the other appliances for the minimum amount of time you can. Hot water; if you have an electric emersion heater, then switch it on for one hour only. The washing machine, use only with a full load and on a cool wash. Items such as dishwashers and tumble dryers, if you have them, do not use. These are expensive luxury items. Wash up the dishes by hand, and air-dry your clothes. The old-fashioned rack my mother used was excellent. Loaded up, it was pulled up to the kitchen ceiling, tied aloft, and worked perfectly, and it cost not one penny to use. You can make one of these for a few pounds.

Microwave ovens are good, quick and cheap to use. Coffee machines are not cheap, and the refills are very expensive. Just buy and use instant coffee if you can afford it.

You all now will be getting the picture of the procedure ahead. Just use all your appliances for the minimum amount of time. And it will reduce your bills.

Gas appliances, mainly these will be your oven or stove and your gas boiler.

On the whole, using gas is considerably cheaper than electricity. The same rules apply here, however. That is use for the minimum amount of time.

Turn the thermostat down as much as you can stand in the winter. Wrap up warm and save, save, save. And remember that central heating uses a lot of gas; only heat your essential rooms – that's the main living room and the bathroom, not your bedrooms.

You must remember that once you're wrapped up in your beds, you'll be snug and warm. Do not use the heating at night while you're sleeping in bed.

These recommendations may seem harsh, but believe me, they work and they will save you money.

I now come to the most extreme and hotly debated cut back of all (THE CAR).

We all have become so accustomed and attached to our cars over the years. The very thought of not having one can make us feel nauseous and breakout into hot sweats.

The sad fact is, however, that the car is one of the most expensive commodities we possess.

You have to make the brutal decision: do I really need this vehicle? Could I or we do without it? No way I hear you cry; it's my best friend; it's even got a name. It's like getting rid of the family dog.

Let's have a look at the pros and cons if you or your partner have a job, even a part-time job. Then you will need the car to commute to and from work. And also if the car is bought and paid for. Then you are in a position to warrant keeping the vehicle.

If, on the other hand, you're on benefits or welfare and your car is on finance, then you are in the sad position; the car has to go.

Of course, if you're disabled, you will need the car to get around. You may also receive some form of assistance to help run the vehicle. Then these are reasons to own a car.

As we all understand, running a vehicle costs money. The costs of driving are high: insurance, road tax, MOT, and fuel and maintenance costs.

Only you and you alone can make this decision, but if your finances are very tight, then you need to make the right decision.

I myself years ago had to make the same decision; I was out of work. For me, it was a sickening decision to make, but it had to be done. Then some months later I wanted to register at a job centre, and I had no money for public transport but was desperate to improve my circumstances. The job centre was about fourteen miles away, so I had no choice but to walk there and back. This walk took me over six hours, twenty-eight miles. It wore a hole in the right shoe of the only pair of shoes I owned. If I had stepped on a fifty pence piece or any other coin, I could have told you if it was heads or tails. I promptly tried to repair it with cardboard. This did not last five minutes, however, in the rain. It makes me laugh when I look back now, but it paid off because four weeks later I was offered a job. And I worked for this company for the next twelve years. Yippee!

Some time later, a friend gave me a pair of boots that he never used. I cleaned them up, greased them, polished them up, and fitted them with new laces. They were a size too big, and I had to wear two pairs of socks, but these boots for country walks and fishing expeditions lasted me for about the next twenty years.

Chapter Four
No Struggle, No Progress

When you have to cut back on all these things through necessity rather than choice, which may well have been the hardest and worst decisions you may have ever experienced. The fact is, though, you will never make any progress without doing so. Once however you have made these decisions and adjustments, you should begin to notice a difference. Life should begin to be a little easier; it ain't no pleasure cruise, but it's not an uphill struggle any more either.

Sometimes we have to lose things to appreciate what we have got. No pain, no gain. And the best method is to think about what you have got rather than what you have not got. And this is not just about material things; most of that stuff means nothing anyway. Always remember that once you work your way up and out of this predicament you are in. Your circumstances will improve dramatically.

Think just how nice it will be to be able to go and buy a new pair of shoes. Buy a new coat; buy another car if you sold the old one. And book a holiday or vacation for you and your family.

All of this now will sound like a pipe dream, but it's nice to dream; it keeps your spirits and hopes up. Never lose sight of those. Without them, you can begin to go under. The very purpose of writing this book is to prevent just that. With hard work and determination, perseverance and guts, things will improve soon. And hopefully you will be on the road to recovery very shortly.

Always bear in mind the principle of rising above the level you are unfortunately at this moment in time. The means to elevate yourself to a better position. The principal here is to make yourself into the most thrifty and resourceful person you have ever imagined yourself to be. To do this, you must capitalise on the most trivial morsels you come across. And to make the most of any opportunity that comes your way and is presented before you. And at all times you must remain within the bounds of the law. Also check out what you are owed.

Always check thoroughly with appropriate departments if you are on benefits or welfare.

Make sure you are getting the correct amount of money you are entitled to.

In the U.K., you can check with citizens advice. They will inform you exactly what you should be receiving from the D.H.S.S. Or the relevant information to get it right.

Universal Credit is what you receive; make sure it's the correct amount; they themselves don't always get it right. And if you're living on a shoestring and a prayer, you need every penny to get by. One pound, £1.00 a week less can be the difference between a meal and nothing.

To any pensioners out there who may be reading this book: and you are not receiving a full state pension; you too should check with pension credit to see if you are eligible for any extra money. There was an enormous amount that was not claimed by pensioners who were entitled to it. In previous years gone by. The princely sum, I believe, was unclaimed. Was in excess of one billion pounds, so do make sure and check with the H.M.R.C. pension department. Have your details with you if you contact them by telephone. N.I. Number, D.O.B., etc., or do it on line.

This money is there to help, so claim what you are entitled to. You have earned it through all your working life.

The upshot here is to make the best out of a bad situation. Easier said than done, I hear you say. That's very true, but just keep your head down and plod on like a cart horse wearing blinkers. Look neither left nor right. Just plod on straight, and you'll get there. Eventually.

Chapter Five
Prudence with Dignity (Make a Stand)

The picture now will be clear to you all: being prudent will now become second nature. What is the definition of being prudent? I hear you ask. Prudence is being as thrifty and conservative as you can possibly be. Counting your pennies and making sure your budget stretches as far as possible. The limited amount of money you have at the moment will soon teach you to become very good. To be perfectly honest, you have no choice. The very fact that you're on a limited budget will create a vacuum around your purse or wallet. You will need to account for every penny you spend, and it will be only on essential items. Prudence was in Victorian times; the lady of the house secretly put away a few pennies every week in a jar towards the family trip to the seaside.

This is the same method and technique you yourselves need to employ; in other words, be careful and as thrifty as you can be.

Let's just take a look at one type of example you may find yourself in.

A typical case in a family is Mum and three kids, just an example. Now Mum being as prudent as she is while the kids are all in school. She has been to the supermarket and had a rummage through the discount section. No shame in this because everybody in this day and age has a look at these bargain items. Even if they don't admit to it. There is nothing wrong with these items; it's just that the supermarkets are covering their own backs getting rid of out-of-sell by date items. It is perfectly good food.

So Mum buys a tin of beans for the discount price of 50p. She knows that at home she has bread and eggs. Her brain is now doing overtime; she has already figured out what is for tonight's tea. Once the kids get home from school, she will serve up her master piece. That is beans on toast with a fried egg on top. This is a great meal for kids; they haven't had their five a day, but they have food in their bellies. Once eaten, they have permission to leave the table and go out to play.

Then dear Ole Mum does the washing up. This will be a typical scenario in millions of households countrywide. Now let's take a close look at the cost.

Prudence being the key factor here, followed by dignity.

Mum finding that tin of beans for the princely sum of 50p. "Well done, Mum."

Dignity being the fact that you have not lost any, everyone takes a peak at the discount section. So you still have all your dignity, no worries.

Cost:
One tin of beans = 50p divided into 4
4 eggs = 80p
4 slices of bread = 8p
Total = 1.38p divided by 4 = 34.5p each

This is the essence of frugality, prudence, and skills that you need to succeed and make it work.

This is just one example that we all can think about.

To all working-class families out there, this procedure will be normal.

Getting by on what you have is an everyday way of life occurrence. It takes tenacity, dedication and skill to make ends meet under these circumstances. It can be done,

It's not easy, but it's not impossible. Just take one day at a time, and you'll make it.

I do remember with sadness and great respect and fondness. A family that lived in close proximity to us. I had some years earlier befriended one of their sons as a mate you hang out with because he was in my class at school. This particular day in the summer holidays, I had eaten my tea and went to call on him to play outside. His brother let me step inside the house. I was greeted by the mother, who informed me that the family was about to have their tea. OK, I said, and as I turned around, I noticed what was on the table for tea. A loaf of bread, a pack of margarine, and one tin of sardines. And this was for a family of six. As I stepped outside, I thought, Blimey Charlie, won't take them long to eat that. Both of the parents worked; the mother was a cleaner, the father was a washer-upper at some hotel. And yet, even the fact that both of them worked, they all were as hard up as that.

The mothers in our neighbourhood were always something very special to us kids.

I observed my own mother going without food to feed us; she would use the excuse I'm not hungry just yet;

maybe I'll have something later. The plain truth was there's nothing later to eat. She went without to feed us. Your mother is the best woman in your life. God bless Ma, R.I.P.

One story I would like to remember to you all was a normal day at school in the woodwork class. My friend from this impoverished family sat next to me in class.

This particular day was sunny, and the woodwork class was as boring as could be, especially with this teacher. He was a vicious and nasty piece of work; in my opinion, now when I look back, he himself should never have been a school teacher.

More like a member of the Gestapo.

As this draining lesson progressed, my friend to my right was preoccupied with the girl's all playing hockey outside the window in their navy blue knickers. Now for young adolescent boys, this is a sight for sore eyes.

Watching all those females romping around outside on the playing fields was far more enjoyable and exciting than woodwork theory.

This appalling teacher soon picked up the fact that we weren't paying attention to his crappy woodwork teachings.

Then, without any hesitation, he let go with a blackboard duster. This, for those of you who don't know, is a solid piece of wood covered in felt. These were used to clean off the chalk from the black boards the teacher used to write upon learning your A.B.C.s, etc.

This projectile hit my friend full square in his forehead; he then turned to me and asked, "How does it look?"

I replied, "Not too good, mate."

With blood trickling down his forehead, he said, "I'm going to get my mum." With that, he got up and walked out. The teacher tried to stop him but to no avail.

Within the next half hour, I knew things would get much more interesting than the previous hours. A little bit more spicy than the rest of the morning.

My friend's mother was a solid type of woman, no nonsense type, who didn't suffer fools kindly. She was the same as most around our neighbourhood. They worked hard; they were loving mothers; they thought the world of their children, maybe not too much of their husbands. And woe be tide to any man that would threaten their youngsters.

The corridor along this section of the school had four fire doors, very heavy doors obviously to stop a fire. After about half an hour we heard a crump, then five minutes later, another crump, but this time more fierce, more powerful, then five minutes more.

Another crash, accompanied by voices, then the final crash, which seemed to bring the walls down. There was lots of shouting; I knew full well this was my friend's mother.

The class room door flew open like a hurricane had arrived. The teacher was sitting in his chair, and the head teacher was trying in vain, a futile gesture, to calm down my friend's mother. Within seconds, the teacher had lost the collar off his shirt. The sheer force of the woman had sent him reeling over the table, crashing into the rubbish bins on the floor beyond. Of course all of us watching in class were amused and applauding every moment of what we witnessed that day in school.

The mothers here were diamonds; they were solid, dependable, we all talked both girls and boys about the happenings of what took place that day.

We all used to refer to them as she bears with cubs, very dependable, very strong, and not to be fooled with.

I can to this day honestly say that it was the best piece of real theatre drama I've ever seen and witnessed. Amazing stuff; even the headmaster got a slap; his glasses flew across the room.

The nasty, vicious teacher, the gestapo officer, crawled out from under his desk. Very soon afterward, took early retirement to everyone's relief.

My friend's mother's name was Veronica; she was nicknamed Vinegar Vera.

And she remained a heroine to us all forever. No charges were ever brought forward by either party, but that's how it was back in 1960s England. People took care of their own and minded their own business.

Food Banks

Food banks and other charities are not to be overlooked because most local councils, and charities and some churches all set aside a day or two to help people who are struggling with the cost of living.

The problem with these stations is the stigma they seem to carry and give people.

The very thought to some people of going into these places fills them with dread.

The main thing to remember here is that bag of provisions that you are given can and will make all the difference.

Many people from all walks of life use these food banks now. This cost of living crisis is the worst many people have ever experienced.

There is no shame in using and accepting help from these stations; they are set up by friendly types who very often have been in the same boat at some point in their lives.

They themselves understand the feelings that people get when going into these establishments.

So do not worry about anything or anyone; just go in and get your bag.

Remember to swallow your pride. All the people inside are the same as you. You are all on the same level; you are all reading off the same page.

So you can see there is no difference, so go ahead and use them; they are there to help. If you are in poor financial shape, then the choices are few. Remember, desperate.

Circumstances require decisive actions, and desperate people do desperate things.

So go ahead, go in and you'll be fine.

Chapter Six
Frugal Recipes

Before we begin to discuss this subject, which is one of the most important when we consider how things are at the moment. The subject of food has to be given a very high degree of priority.

Gone, sadly, at least for the moment, are the days when people could eat out two or three times a week. When takeout meals were the normal part of everyday life.

For anyone this day and age, eating out at restaurants and the prices these establishments command needs serious consideration when they give you the bill at the end of the meal.

These are prices that are beyond the scope and reach of anyone reading this book.

The exorbitant prices for takeout food, i.e., a takeaway curry for two people, £28.00.

This is a colossal amount of money to spend on just one meal.

Along with frugality and cooking skilfully, you should be able to survive all week on that amount of money.

So the message is obviously clear to you all: keep well away from these establishments.

Pizza joints, hamburger joints, fast chicken restaurants, etc. All now should become no-go zones. You simply don't have the money to waste on these types of foods.

The four basic staple ingredients that are essential for cheap meals.
1) potatoes
2) pasta
3) rice
4) bread

These simple and cheap ingredients can and will bulk up your dishes so all of you feel that there is something in your stomachs when you leave the table.

These four basic ingredients I've used many times in many different ways.

They should every week be on your shopping list; try always to have them in your kitchen.

In praise of leftovers:

These leftovers were always put to good use and got eaten up in the old days.

The problem now is that when cooking on such a tight budget, very often you have no leftovers because you will have consumed everything you've cooked.

The message, however, is simple and straightforward: do not waste or throw anything away. If you have any morsel of food left over, save it for later; it will get eaten up at a later date, guaranteed.

Going back to being resourceful and making a meal with leftovers is easier than you might think. You will learn how to stretch out what you've got.

Cooking is enjoyable, and you know at the end, you'll have something nice to eat.

I kept my own hens for a lot of years – decades – in fact, a great thing to have because with your own hens and fresh eggs and a sack of potatoes, you always have a potential meal on tap. Egg and chips. Potato omelette, to name just two.

I remember some years back when one of my hens had a brood of youngsters, chicks.

I had let them out for a few hours free-ranging. Very important to Mum and family, she teaches them many things – what's good to eat and what's not.

I had a small handful of cooked leftover rice, too little to do much with. And my waste not want, not theory in life, not even one grain. I threw it in some long grass for Ma, as I called her, to find with her brood. She went into that grass full steam ahead with all the youngsters trolling behind her. Lots of cackling and bubbling came from that grass patch; she was telling them, Look, kids, this ere is good to eat.

I went out about an hour later and took a look at what had happened to this handful of rice. I wasn't surprised that Ma had removed every single grain of it from the grass. Not one single grain remaining, and the chicks were all now drinking dew drops off blades of grass quenching their thirst. Sipping the dew, like champagne. AHH!

I thought what genius that was – how resourceful animals are to utilise every single grain. And we call them dumb animals. It's not them that's dumb; it's us.

Think how much food we throw away. It's a sin and a crime; it could feed an army of people or animals. So be resourceful and think like Ma.

Public enemy number one: supermarkets.

It has to be said that the big conglomerate stores and supermarkets have their cake and eat it. They control the markets where all goods and produce originate.

They even control the farmers, who work very hard to produce our food.

They dictate everything, from what prices they pay to our farmers. They have the power to cancel at a moment's notice, and the farmers have lost whole fields of produce and receive no compensation.

With the development of the war in Ukraine, all these supermarkets are guilty of putting prices up; they charge people what they want. They try to put it across and give the impression that they are bending over backwards to keep all their prices as low as possible. I don't believe one word of it. They all are profiteering from this situation in Ukraine. One example is tinned tomatoes; now Spain, Italy, and the Netherlands all produce vast quantities of tomatoes. The Ukraine does not; Italy produces the most tomatoes by far, which end up in tins. How then can these supermarkets justify the price increase of 100% from 30p a year ago to today's price of 60p a tin?

There is no excuse to warrant an increase of that magnitude.

Let it be said that these greedy grasping and exorbitant supermarkets are using the Ukraine war as an excuse for profiteering.

They care only about three things. Profit, profit, and more profit. Enough said.

Good, honest vegetables:

Let's all take a look at one of our best friends in the kitchen, vegetables.

Honest to goodness, vegetables. Frankly, I can't praise them enough.

They are an amazing, excellent source of food for very little cost.

If you go shopping with just £10.00, or $10.00, for example, and you want to buy meat, then that amount of money will not buy you much meat. You will be able to carry the meat home in your pocket.

However, if you go shopping with the same amount of money and you want to purchase vegetables. Then you will need a wheelbarrow to bring it all back home.

An excellent source of vitamins and minerals, incorporate vegetables in your daily diet at every given opportunity.

If you are lucky enough to have access to your own garden, then, if possible, section off a patch so you can grow and plant some vegetables of your own.

It is without doubt a marvellous thing to grow your own, go out and lift a few spuds.

Cut a cabbage and return to the kitchen and cook them for tea.

This veggie patch only takes work to create and very little money.

If you can possibly create one, then do it; you won't be disappointed.

Although I've grown my own for many years, I'll refrain from going into great detail about it, techniques, situations and planting, etc. It's all beyond the scope of this book.

Just have a go if you can, and you'll be amazed at what you can achieve.

Foraging:

Again, springtime is for me the best time of year to go outdoors and search for edibles that are totally free. These fresh spring greens are a real treat and something to look forward to. Unconsidered morsels, which most people step over and consider as mere weeds, are, in fact, the very essence of the most nutritious food you can put on your plate.

Again, in this limited-scope small book, I'll give you just three examples of what you can gather outside in the woods and fields, take home and use for a meal.

1) Wild garlic, onion family, alliums. Great in salads, pesto, soups and sauces,

I eat the white flowers in May, a fantastic lunch, tomato salad, garlic flowers, bread, cheese, and a glass of wine. Excellent, delicious, cheap and good for you. The whole plant is edible; the leaves are first, then the buds, then the flowers.

2) Nettles, dreaded by schoolboys falling into them. Me being one many times.

Dreadful, fearful plants that you all avoid have nasty stings.

From the culinary point of view, these plants, however, have more vitamins and mineral nutrients than any other plant in the world. (pick the tops only.)

Super food: when springtime comes, I always make a green spring superfood soup.

Of wild garlic and nettle and hogweed shoots. It costs pennies to make. I'll make this soup about three times while the plants last. Then, as spring approaches summer, the bounty sadly dies out. You then have to wait for a full year for the plants to come back into reproduction. Something to look forward to.

3) Hog weed shoots.

These I use as spring greens; for me, they are like asparagus, lovely just steamed and tossed in garlic butter. They have a lovely flavour of their own, like cardamom, plenty of garlic, and lemon juice, and salt. Fantastic.

Again, I've only given you three plants that can make a great addition and difference to your meal times. Do make absolutely sure that you know what you're eating.

There are plenty of plants out there that you can eat.

There are also plenty of plants out there that you can't eat.

Make sure you get expert advice; buy a book on foraging; better still, go out with an expert forager, somebody who knows what's what.

There are plants out there that look very appetising, fresh and green; one that comes to mind is Hemlock water drop wort. This plant is deadly poisonous and, if consumed, will have you lying on a slab within twelve hours with a tag on your toe. Deceased.

For the love of homemade soup.

These simple recipes for delicious homemade soups are some of my favourites I've made over the years. They are very underrated, but yet easy to make, very nutritious, and as cheap as chips.

A full bowl of steaming hot homemade soup on a winter's day or any other day for that matter will be a sight for sore eyes or a delight to behold. Accompanied with a large chunk of fresh baked bread.

These soups go well for a light lunch, but for your evening meal you will need something more substantial. Once you've cooked and eaten homemade soup,

You will never buy tin soups at exorbitant prices ever again.

1st, this is my favourite; all four of these soups are amazing, delicious, and so tasty.

1) Onion Soup with a Floating Cheese Crouton

Ingredients (serves four people)
2 or 3 onions, sliced.
1 potato, peeled and diced.
2 cloves of garlic, chopped.

1 stock pot, or cube, chicken, optional.
Water. Oil, seasoning, bread and cheese.

Method

Fry the onions and garlic until transparent. (Do not burn)
Add the potato.
Add the water and stock if using.
Simmer until tender, about 15/20 minutes.
You want a consistency here like double cream.
The potato will thicken the soup, or use flour and water mixed to thicken.
Check the seasoning, salt and pepper.
Meantime, cover some bread with cheddar cheese and place under a hot grill.
Once the soup is cooked, blitz with a blender until smooth.
Float the cheese on toast on top, and serve.
This is a very basic version, cheap and quick to make.
You can tweak it with other ingredients, like parsley, chili flakes, whatever takes your fancy, garnish with wild garlic flowers in the spring. Excellent.

2) Green Spring Soup

Ingredients (serves four people)
1 onion,
2 cloves garlic,
1 potato, peeled and diced.
2 large handfuls of wild garlic.
2 large handfuls of nettle tops.
1 bunch of parsley.
1 stock pot or cube, chicken, optional.
Water, oil, seasoning.

Method
Fry the onion and garlic until tender.
Add the potato.
Wash the greens, roughly chop.
Only use the soft tops of the nettles.
Add the parsley.
Add the stock and the water.
Simmer for about 15/20 minutes.
Check the seasoning.
Blitz with a blender till smooth.

Serve hot with crusty bread. A fantastic superfood soup.

3) Celeriac and Mushroom

Ingredients (serves four people)
1 onion
4 cloves garlic.
Half a celeriac root.
Good handful of any mushrooms.
Parsley.
Oil, water and seasoning.

Method
Fry sliced onions with the garlic until soft.
Add peeled and diced celeriac.
Add chopped mushrooms.
Add the parsley.
Top up with plain water.
Simmer until tender, about 20 minutes.
Check the seasoning. And blitz with a blender.
 Garnish with more parsley, and a splash of cream if you have it.
 Again, serve with some bread. Cheap and economical. Scrumptious.

4) Red Pepper and Tomato

Ingredients (serves four people)
2 red peppers.
1 onion.
3 cloves garlic.
1 tin tomatoes.
Parsley.
Chicken stock.
Oil water and seasoning.

Method
Fry off the onions and garlic until tender.
Add the chopped peppers, fry for two minutes.
Add the tomatoes.
Add the parsley.
Add a cup of stock.
Top up with the water.
Cook gently until tender.
Adjust the seasoning; if required, thicken with flour and cold water mix.
Blitz up with a blender,
Garnish with chopped parsley,
Serve hot with some good bread. Delicious.

This is only a small part of the soup recipe collection. You're basically unlimited with the choice of soups you can make. This is where you can make use of any leftovers.

If you need to stretch out any soup if you're a bit short, bulk it up with some pasta or cooked rice. This will be more filling; waste nothing; other soups to make.
Leek and potato.
Tomato.
Pea and ham.
Mulligatawny.
Chicken and mushroom.
Chicken barley broth.
Minestrone.
Celery.
You can even make soup with lettuce; the list goes on; it's endless; do try them all when you can. And you won't be disappointed.

The Humble Potato Sarnie
When things are really tight, and I mean tight. Your skint. This can be a lifesaver.
Potatoes and bread, nowt special in that. It's a chip butty. Well yeah, but with a twist.
Try this, and you'll see the kids will love it.
Slice a large onion and fry until soft. Add a beef stock cube, add some water to make a gravy. Take two slices of any bread you have in the kitchen. Put on any potato you have to hand, mash, fried, chips, even boiled spuds sliced up will do, or roast, make a nice sandwich, season with salt and pepper. Dip into the onion gravy, and enjoy.

Corned Beef Hash with a Crust
Serve with red cabbage.
Serves four people. A good winter warmer.
I remember this was one of my mother's favourites, made special with the thick pastry crust on top, which sometimes she would mix in some mashed potatoes. (leftovers)

Ingredients.
1 tin corned beef. Cubed.
2 potatoes, peeled and chopped.
1 carrot, diced.
1 onion, diced.
2 cloves garlic, chopped.
Beef stock.
Parsley.
water and seasoning.

Method
This is simplicity and cooks itself.
Put all the ingredients in a saucepan; add the stock and parsley.
Simmer gently until cooked, then in the meantime take one large cup of plain flour.
Add a pinch of salt, add water and make a dough. On a floured surface, roll out to about half an inch thick.
When the stew is cooked, transfer to an ovenproof dish. Place the crust over, make a hole in the top, brush with milk, and bake in a medium oven until golden. Serve

up with pickled red cabbage, brown sauce, or both. Delightful.

The baked or jacket potato is a humble and versatile standby when you're on a tight budget. These can serve as a meal for a child, especially when you put their favourite filling into the potato. The fillings you can use are only limited by your own imagination; there are infinite possibilities and choices.
Here are just a few, basically whatever the kids like.
Sweet corn and mayonnaise.
Baked beans.
Grated cheese.
Fried bacon bits.
Cooked ham.
Flaked smoked haddock
Savoury minced meat.
Cooked sausage.
Hard-boiled egg, etc.
As you can see, the list of ingredients is endless. Use medium- or large-sized potatoes. Clean them, rub them with oil, and bake in a medium oven for about one and a half hours until soft. Cut them open and add a knob of butter and salt and anything else that you fancy.
And if the kids eat the skins so much, the better because they get the fibre and vitamins.
Always remember when using your oven to utilise the empty space with another dish.
For example, a rice pudding, two dishes for the price of one.

Pasta and Tomatoes
This is another good cheap recipe.
Cook pasta for as many as needed. Spaghetti, tagliatelle, macaroni, fusilli, or Penne.
If you slice and fry an onion until soft, it makes this pasta dish more appetising.
Mix the cooked onion with the pasta and add a tin of chopped tomatoes.
Simply heat through in a saucepan, and if you have them, add grated cheese on top and sprinkle with some chopped parsley. Meatballs or any meat leftovers go well with this, if you have any.

Cottage Pie
Or shepherd's pie if using lamb.

Ingredients (serves four)
1 lb or half a kilo minced beef/lamb.
4 potatoes.
1 onion, sliced.
1 clove garlic,. chopped.
Seasoning.

Method
Peel and cook the potatoes. In salted water until tender, then make mashed potatoes.
Add a drop of milk and a knob of butter and season well. Set aside.

Fry the onion and garlic until tender, add the minced beef fry until the mince takes on a bit of colour. About two minutes.
Put into an ovenproof dish, and top with the mashed potato.
Bake in a moderate oven, gas 4, 190°C, for about 40 minutes or until the top is golden and crispy.
If you have any spare cheese, even the rind will do; grate some over the top before putting in the oven.
Serve with a green vegetable.
Remember, if you have the ingredients, add another dish to the oven and cook this at the same time. Like this next recipe.

Homemade Rice Pudding

Ingredients (serves four)
3 cups of pudding rice.
1 pint of milk.
1 pint water. For economy.
Nutmeg, if you have any.
1 cup sugar.

Method
Grease an ovenproof dish with butter or margarine.
Add the rice.
Add the sugar.
Add the milk and water.
Stir until the sugar dissolves.
Dot with butter.

Grate or sprinkle with nutmeg if using.

Bake in the oven for about one hour, maybe a bit longer, until a skin forms on top and the pudding is set.

Medium heat oven, gas 4 190°C.

Put this in the oven first; half an hour later, the cottage pie. So they cook together. For example.

And they both finish at the same time.

Better rice pudding than anything out of a tin. Good with homemade jam.

Sausage Casserole. Pork or Beef

Ingredients (serves four)
4 sausages one each, 8 sausages two each, if you're prosperous.
A few mushrooms, chopped.
1 onion, sliced.
2 cloves garlic, chopped.
1 tin of chopped tomatoes.
Parsley.
Seasoning.

Method
Fry the sausages until they have some colour.
Fry the onion and garlic together until tender, with the mushrooms.
Transfer to an ovenproof dish.
Season with salt and pepper.
Add the tomatoes.

Stir well and cook in a moderate oven for an hour; don't let it get too dry.
Serve with mashed potato.
Sprinkle with chopped parsley. One of my son's favourites, and particularly filling.

At the time of writing this book, one local butcher's shop was selling a full chicken for £4.00. About $5.00 approximately, how many meals can you get from a full chicken?
Let's have a good look at this one.
If you are prosperous enough in the first place to afford a full chicken. And I hope you all are.
1) Let us say that we are for Sunday dinner having roast chicken with all or some of the trimmings. WOW, what a treat.
2) After the roast chicken dinner, for four individuals, i.e., Mum, Dad, and two kids, most of the breast meat and legs will be eaten. What you have left is a full carcass, which can be stretched out to make more meals.
Sadly, this day and age, you do not have the giblets inside you had in the old days.
I shed a tear at its passing; these items inside were a valuable addition to a chicken.
You could stretch it even further with the giblets, making soup, stock, and pate.
Nevertheless, you can still do well with what you have left.

For the kids' tea tomorrow, pick the carcass of meat and chicken wings, serve up chicken and chips,
3) The rest of the meat, if any, throw into an omelette, with onions and potatoes to bulk it up.
4) The whole carcass now goes into a pot with onions, garlic, carrots, potatoes, celery,
And pearl barley, and a stock cube. And is simmered up for an hour or more to produce the best chicken broth you have ever tasted. Very nourishing and made from leftovers.

This is the best way to make the most of what you have; do not waste anything.
And remember, even when it's all been eaten up, give the remains to the cat.
I am positive and sure the cat will appreciate it greatly. My own cats loved anything like this; they would munch away on the bones until everything was consumed.

Mincemeat Stew and Dumplings
This is another one-pot recipe, very easy, simple, delicious and economical to make.

Ingredients (serves four people)

1 lb or half kilo of minced beef.
2 onions.
2 cloves of garlic.
1 carrot.
1 potato.
Half a cabbage.

2 sticks of celery.
Stock pot or cube, beef.
Parsley.
Seasoning.

Method
Fry off the onions and garlic until transparent; add the mince; cook for another 2 minutes; add the rest of the vegetables, parsley, stock, and seasoning.
Top up with some water, enough to cover the ingredients.
Simmer for about 30 minutes.
In the meantime, for the dumplings, put the flour in a bowl and add the salt. Add enough cold water to make a dough. Add some chopped parsley and form into golf ball-size shapes. Set aside.

Parsley Dumplings

Ingredients
Use 1 cup of self-raising flour.
Pinch of salt.
Water to mix.

After about 30 minutes of cooking, place the dumplings on top of the stew; the self-raising flour will swell up and cover the whole stew. Cook for another 20 minutes, and it's done.
Delicious. Serve up with pickled red cabbage.

Banana Milk Shakes and Smoothies
These smoothies are a meal in themselves, good for a breakfast before the kids go to school. Some people may be concerned about using a raw egg.
I've drank hundreds of these shakes over the years and never had any problems.
If you use good eggs, you will be fine. If you're worried, omit the egg. You will need a blender to make them smooth.

Per person.
1 banana. Peeled.
1 egg.
Half a pint of milk.
Sugar to taste.

Method
Place all in the blender and blitz up till smooth and enjoy.

Pulses.
These are another good cheap staple to use in your cooking to make your meals stretch as far as possible. All of these pulses below are excellent.

Dried.
Split peas.
Haricot beans.
Butter beans.

All these types of dried peas and beans need to be pre-soaked, preferably overnight.
Barley, although not a pulse, being a grain (does not need soaking), I have included in this section.

Haricot Bean Soup

Ingredients (serves four people)
Half a kilo beans, soaked.
2 onions.
1 pint of water.
Half a pint of milk.
Table spoon plain flour.
Knob of butter.
Seasoning.

Method
Put the soaked beans into a saucepan with the onions, seasoning and water.
Bring to the boil, then simmer 1 hour.
Blend the flour with the milk until smooth.
Add to the soup.
Cook on a low heat until the right consistency. Blitz with a blender.
This soup goes well with bacon.
Add the butter, serve with fried croutons.

Bacon and Bean Casserole

Ingredients (serves four people)

Half kilo dried butter beans (soaked)
Ham shank, or forehock, knuckle. Also works well with a lamb shank.
4 tomatoes.
1 green pepper.
2 carrots.
1 stick of celery.
1 onion.
1 clove garlic.
1 litre water.
Stock pot, chicken cube.
Seasoning.

Method

This dish is cooked slowly in a moderate oven, gas 3, 150° C for 2 hours and 30 minutes.
Goes well with jacket potatoes, cooked alongside.
Keep the ham shank or foreknuckle on the bone for more flavour.
Put the ham and beans in an ovenproof dish.
Slice the pepper and tomatoes.
Chop up the carrots, onion and celery.
Place all in the casserole dish.
Seasoning well.
Add water and stock.
Cover and cook in a moderate oven 2.5hrs.
Remember if using to add the jacket potatoes after the first hour of cooking. Excellent.

Lentils.
Red, green and black.
All these are good choices; no need to soak.
Lentil soup is very good; Asian spiced lentil Dal is also good.
These can be added to soups and stews to bulk them up and stretch them out to feed more people if required.

Lentil Soup

Ingredients (serves four people)

Half kilo lentils.
2 potatoes, peeled and diced.
2 onions, sliced.
2 sticks of celery, chopped.
2 cloves garlic, chopped.
1 litre of water.
1 cup milk.
Mixed herbs.

Method
Place all the ingredients in a saucepan with the seasoning and a good pinch of mixed herbs.
Bring to the boil and simmer until tender. About 40 minutes.
Allow to cool some, and blitz with a blender.
Add the milk, stir and serve with bread. Garnish with chopped parsley.

Egg and Leek Bake

Ingredients (serves four people)

4 potatoes. Peeled and diced.
4 large leeks, chopped.
8 hard-boiled eggs.
500g mashed potato.
300 ml of warm milk.
1 tablespoon flour.
2 tablespoons butter.
50g grated cheese.
Plus a bit more.
Seasoning.

Method
Boil the potatoes in salt water until tender, then make about 500g mashed potatoes.
Boil the leeks in salt water for about ten minutes; drain well.
Add the leeks to the mash, season well and add half the butter; mix all together.
Place into an ovenproof dish.
Heat the rest of the butter, add the flour and the warm milk, stir well, avoiding lumps and add half the cheese.
Cut the eggs in half and place into the centre of the dish.
Inside the leek and potato mixture.
Cover with the cheese sauce, sprinkle over the remaining cheese.

Bake in the oven gas 6, 200c, until the top is golden brown. About half an hour.

Egg-fried Rice and Tuna

Ingredients (serves four people)
Cooked rice for four people.
4 eggs.
2 tins tuna fish, drained.

This makes a quick breakfast or lunch; it's filling and nutritious.

Method
Take a wok or frying pan, heat some oil and fry half the quantity of the rice.
Fry for about 3 or 4 minutes, stirring all the time. Add 2 eggs and keep stirring.
Then add the tuna fish, seasoning, stir a bit more and serve. Then repeat.

The price of fish:
You only have to take a walk around a fishmonger's slab or market stall.
In this day and age, the prices of fish are breathtaking. What a shame because fish years ago was affordable. Now it's as expensive as meat, if not more so. Shellfish too is up there on the same level.

So for this reason, I've only included two recipes in this book. As I feel that the cost will sadly be beyond the reach of most people who are reading this.

There is one cheap way to incorporate at least some fish into your diet, and that is to eat two tins of sardines or tuna fish every week. Or two of each if you can afford it.

That way you will at least be eating some fish. Basically, there are two types of fish out there. Whitefish, and Bluefish.

1) Whitefish, Cod, Haddock, Plaice, Ling, Flounder, etc. These are the most expensive.

Types of fish, but the most popular.

2) Bluefish, Mackerel, Herring, Sardines, etc, are cheap and oily and better for you. Also, you have salmon, trout, and fresh tuna, but these also are very expensive. Considering that we in the U.K. are Islanders and surrounded by sea, you would think that the price of fish would be lower. We all know that our fishermen have to make a living.

And appreciate that they do a very important and dangerous job bringing the fish back home. Good luck to all at sea.

Pan-fried Mackerel Fillets

Ingredients (serves four people)
4 mackerel = 8 fillets.
New potatoes.
Garden peas.

Horseradish sauce.

You can buy these cheap when they are in season and plentiful.
Ask your fishmonger to fillet them for you, and keep the scraps for the cat if you have one.

Method
Simply pan fry in oil until cooked through, only 3/4 minutes.
Put your potatoes on first and cook in salted water until tender. Drain and keep warm.
In the same pan add the peas. Cook for 3/4 minutes,
Fry the mackerel fillets at the same time.
Serve with the horseradish sauce.

Fish cakes:
If ever you do have any leftover fish, mix with mashed potatoes, flakes of white fish, chopped onions, parsley, and seasoning. Fry on both sides until golden and crispy.
Serve with chips or French fries and mayonnaise. Nice.

Bubble and Squeak:
Again, this delicacy made from leftover cabbage or Brussels sprouts and mashed potatoes is a kid's favourite. Just mix together equal amounts of cooked cabbage, or Brussels sprouts, and mashed potatoes. Season well, and fry on both sides until golden and

crispy, preferably in some butter or bacon grease. Serve hot with chutney or sauce.

The name, by the way, comes from the noise it makes while cooking. It bubbles and it squeaks.

Rissoles/ Patties.
Chopped meat – anything will do.
Lamb, beef, pork, bacon, ham, chicken, corned beef – again leftovers if you have some.
Mix with mashed potatoes, chopped meat, and a little chopped onion, parsley and seasoning. Fry on both sides until golden in butter, bacon fat, or better yet, beef dripping. Serve hot with chips or French fries and chutney.
A teatime special treat for the kids. Priceless.

Potato cakes.
These are good for breakfast, very cheap, good with a fried egg on top.
Again, mashed potatoes, some flour, melted butter, seasoning,
Use up the old, floury potatoes for the best results.
Take your mash, add some melted butter, and stir in a tablespoon of flour, and season well. Mix all together and form into round balls or patties. Squash down to flatten.
Fry until golden brown on both sides and serve with a fried egg on top.

Dripping on toast.

This was when I was a child, acted as a keep-us-going snack when we came home from school before tea. Unfortunately, this delicacy rarely seems to be eaten by the children these days. They don't know what they are missing.

It was simply made from the essence of meat in a roasting tin or pan. Any meat would do, but beef was the best.

Take 1 slice of hot buttered toast and spread with the brown jelly essence from the bottom of the pan. Then sprinkle with a pinch of salt, and eat. WOW!

As you all can see now, these frugal recipes came from hard times. Resourceful people who experienced these times from a distant past bygone era. Unfortunately for us, they have returned with vengeance.

It never ceases to amaze me how much ingenuity and tenacity people can find when they have to. How families can pull together, help each other out, and feed their own,

This is what we have and all know as kinship. And I must say it makes me proud to belong to humble working-class people. God bless them.

Chapter Seven
A Road to Nowhere

"The world is a dangerous place, not because of those who do evil. But because of those who look on and do nothing."
– Albert Einstein.

The best thing I can say here is, one step at a time, one thing at a time, and one day at a time. When you're on the road to nowhere, you are walking in circles and making no progress; you are coming back on yourself, right back to square one.

The feeling of being alone in the world, despair, sadness, and isolation are all very normal feelings when an individual is down on their luck. Things just don't seem to work out right; desperation and fear are some of the feelings you experience on a daily basis.

Take my word for it, you are not alone in this world; there's thousands out there who are in the same boat. You feel anger and anxiety; it wakes you up in the middle of the night with thoughts of what if it gets worse? How long will this last for? The factual truth here is you don't know. How long is a piece of string? Your fate hangs in the balance; your fate is in God's hands.

What did I do to deserve or warrant this.? The plain fact is nothing; you are passing through a dark tunnel, a bad phase in your life, which I believe everybody has to pass through so as to prove their worth. This journey you are on will and does sort the men out from the boys. It's as though you are being assessed and watched by a force from above. And the tougher you are, the harder your test will be.

All I know is that the truth is the truth, and it always stays the same.

People experience these times, some more than others, some longer than others, some harder than others. And some never at all. The very meaning or reason or purpose behind this phenomenon, I've not quite yet figured it out, but I'm sure there is one.

As stated in an earlier chapter, I'm not a religious person, but I do believe in a God up there somewhere, hopefully.

It does hold mind-boggling possibilities of what is out there. What my point is, do we find out the real truth after we pass away? Do we really pass on to a different realm? Is there another dimension that we travel through to discover another life after this life is over?

Or is death just that and nothing more?

Many people who are struggling in this cost of living crisis have never experienced this kind of hardship before. For some years now, people have had a false sense of security with very low interest rates. A kind of false money that will exist for ever and a day and for years to come. As we all have realised after the COVID pandemic and the cost of living crisis, this false economy has now collapsed and come to a standstill. Interest rate rises one after another are like a noose around your neck getting tighter month by month. In the late 1970s, the interest rate rose, then quadrupled the mortgages people had on their homes. I remember a friend hanging on by the skin of his teeth to keep his home. It was a worrying time for everyone. For those of you now who are in that predicament, you all have my full sympathies.

At the time of writing this, there will be another interest rate rise this week. The present government is trying hard to bring inflation down, but it won't be easy. There is nothing more certain; it will get harder before it gets better.

What this means is that this cost of living crisis will run for at least another two years.

This is the very reason I am writing this book. Unfortunately, there is no easy solution or remedy; there is no easy way out; there is no easy escape. You just have to grit your teeth and hunker down, and hang on and cope the best way you can.

In the previous chapters, I've written as much as my experiences allow to get you all through these difficult times. I do very much hope that I have made a difference.

The upshot here and the end game is that you yourselves are the only ones that make the difference. You yourselves are the only ones who make it work. Without your own inner strength and tenacity, you will fail.

There is no such thing as a free lunch; it does not matter one jot who is in government.

In the U.K., the Conservative Party, or the Labour Party, or in the U.S.A. The Democrats, or the Republicans, doesn't matter; you and only you can and will make the difference.

Keep enough fuel in your tank, don't overshoot, plod on, and plough on, and at the end, when things begin to get better, you will walk out the other side a proud man or woman.

And begin to have a helluva time living your life to the fullest.

I must now briefly cover the distasteful subject of habits and vices.

This subject has to be discussed and looked at carefully, if only in minuscule detail.

We all know that habits and vices can and do affect our finances. The only way we can make progress here is to control what we have and do. In other words, limit what we do and spend or stop all together. *Ha ha*, I hear you say.

The plain fact here is if you have one or more of these habits or vices and you don't have them under control. Then your prospects and future are bleak.

You will never pull yourself out of the mire and the mud. You will remain weak and vulnerable; you will remain where you are or sink and go under.

1) Gambling.
2) Drugs.
3) Tobacco.
4) Alcohol.

All of the above can and will cause major problems and upset to anyone who is in your family, friends, or associates who you spend time with or share your life with. If you have a problem with any or more of the above, you must get a grip of the situation. If you cannot do this yourself, then you must get professional help and advice.

Smoking, for example, we all know the dangers here; at this present moment in time in the U.K., a 20 pack of cigarettes costs £14.10p. So if someone smokes 20 a day, that's

£98.70p a week. Nobody in dire straits can afford to spend that amount of money on a product that's literally killing you.

Gambling – this is a serious addiction that can ruin your life. It's a mugs game; do yourself a big favour and stop. If you can't get help. Drugs and alcohol – the cost here depends on what you are on and how much you consume. Only you will know the answer to this. Whatever the case is here, if you have a problem, go forward and get help. Of course I know when people are under pressure and stress, some will turn to these substances for relief from the depressive life they lead.

The plain fact is none of the above help the situation; they make it one hundred times worse. So be your own best friend, not your worst enemy, and seek help from within yourself if you can. If you can't get professional help and advice.

Suicide or Bust:

This is probably one of the most difficult topics, if not the most unapproachable and unsavoury subjects in this book. I do feel, however, that the stigma of suicide, the lack of awareness about this subject, and the sweep it under the carpet attitude that seems to surround this subject need to be addressed. One of those subjects you wouldn't bring up for conversation at the dinner party table.

I think that when your world seems to come crashing down around you. You lose hope in your life, and you wonder why you're really here at all.

There are many reasons why these symptoms can happen and come about to make you feel that you cannot carry on any more with this life.

The feeling of blackness and despair that crawls into your soul, like you don't belong to anything or anybody. The only friend you have is the Devil himself, or his henchmen Lucifer or Satan, and you are totally alone in a world of darkness and evil.

That there is no chance that you will recover from these terrible times of sadness.

That the only way to escape these terrible depths of deprivation and hopelessness is to end it all by taking your own life and thus take the pain away.

I can describe these symptoms because I've had them myself.

There is no doubt it's a dreadful place to be, especially if you're alone.

Some years ago I spent sixteen years living abroad in Europe, living the dream of a life of self-sufficiency. It went well for some years until my income dried up.

After some time of not having any income, I decided to approach the social services for some assistance while I looked for work. They informed me that as a single male I was low priority, and as I had not contributed any money into the system, I was not entitled to any help. I knew then

I was about to embark upon the most difficult times in my life.

For the next eighteen months, I survived living off the land. I ate things that would make a dog throw up. Frogs, snakes, rabbits peeled off the road.

Chestnuts, berries, nuts, worms and wood lice, etc. I wondered around all day gathering edibles like Neanderthal man. At the beginning, my weight was eleven stone, about 155 pounds.

After eighteen months, my weight was 5.5 stone, about 77 pounds.

All my top teeth dropped out through malnutrition.

When the doctor gave me an examination, he remarked you could have been in a prison camp. I then did receive some help from social services and found some work.

My point here in telling you all this is that no matter how low in your life, you sink.

There is always hope around the corner; never in these times did I ever consider or contemplate suicide. I consider this an insult to your own mother, who carried you for nine months and then delivered you into the world by a painful childbirth to live your life. Not to take it away.

If you get wiped out in a war or die in a R.T.A. Run over by an eighteen wheeler, hit by a train, or flattened by a bus. Then, so be it, things happen in life. This is a natural state of affairs, tragic as it is. Suicide is not. My survival instinct is very strong, and committing suicide is not survival. Preachers can talk about self-pity, but I don't agree with suicide.

To me, there is no greater form of self-pity.

Live now and die later; you are a long time dead. I owed it to myself and my mother. R.I.P. Ma!

This is what I think about suicide; if people reading this book disagree, then that is your point of view. Every man is entitled to his own point of view, and this one is mine.

All walks of life can and do experience these challenges in this day and age, although it is normally the working classes who endure these obstacles and difficulties. The upper classes hardly ever experience such times, but what has come to light in recent years is the fact that some of the middle classes are going through hard times themselves. Some of them are now using food banks and are in arrears with their mortgages. It just goes to show how severe this cost of living crisis is.

Always keep in mind the fact that one of these days things will take a turn for the better. It may well seem a very long way off now, but seeing is believing.

Just this week, after fourteen consecutive interest rate hikes, the Bank of England has announced that this month the rate will remain unchanged. Wow wonders will never cease. And ironically, this week is also the first anniversary of Liz Truss and Kwasi Kwarteng's disastrous mini-budget. That drove a coach and horses through the economy and ran it straight off a cliff. Shambolic is the word for it. I think we all have a long way to go yet, but let's all live in hope that the tide is beginning to turn and the future will begin to shine just that little bit brighter for all of us very soon.

Chapter Eight
The Road to Recovery

Yeah, it's the road to recovery. We are now walking along. Welcome to everybody. The hardest times have finally passed us by. Do not, however, celebrate too quickly because we have a long journey ahead. Finally, there is a little glimmer of light at the end of the tunnel, which we all have been looking forward to seeing for so long.

It is a plain fact of life that the good times can and do come to an end.

It is also a fact of life that the bad times can and will come to an end. This ending is now turning into a new chapter, a new beginning.

Your guts and determination, forward planning, and endless endurance will pull you through all of this and put an end to this nonsense once and for all.

Many people out there who have been through this struggle before will know that the time for celebrating is a long way off. It may take years to get yourself back to normal, but the purpose of this book is to get you all through the most difficult and challenging times. That is my job; the rest is up to you.

When things do eventually start to pick up, circumstances will change fast, so keep your running shoes to hand and get ready to move with the times. We all have had enough of being down in the doldrums; we are now committed to change for the better.

The future now will begin to look just that bit more promising, and you will do your utmost to make it happen.

These distressing events of hunger, poverty and want may mean that you could be suffering somewhat from mental health issues. Depression could be a symptom of isolation, feeling alone, and antisocial behaviour or wanting to be by yourself more frequently than normal. Do not despair because these symptoms are all related to your situation and relative by degree to how badly these past experiences have affected you and your family.

Post-traumatic stress disorder, or P.T.S.D. This condition can affect different people in different ways depending on the individual.

Always remember the fact that you are now beginning to ascend out of these difficulties, and therefore these challenging circumstances can and will be put behind you. Do not dwell in the past; think like animals do and forget the past and look forward to tomorrow. What's gone by yesterday and today is just that, GONE. Your future will begin to improve soon enough, but make sure you are prepared and ready to accept it and take it on. If you condition yourself in this way, you will be fine, and you will do well.

Let us now look at what can really make a big difference to changing your miserable circumstances into a positive experience and a healthy lifestyle that you and your family will enjoy. There are three words to describe what can and will make the difference to change your life around, for good, permanently.

JOB. JOB. JOB.

GET ONE NOW.

The sooner this happens, the sooner you will be on this road to recovery. At this moment in time, there are many thousands of jobs out there just waiting for you to take them on.

Many employers in the U.K. are desperate to find people; this means that you can cherry pick and choose what suits your best interests. If you are on benefits and you are receiving Universal Credit, for example, you can also work for three days a week to help supplement your income. This is the maximum they allow you to work, i.e., twenty four hours, so for example, Dad may find this suitable, and it could well lead to a better full-time job. Yippee.

On the other hand, for Mum, this could be too many hours, so she could work for just four hours a day. For example, she could take the kids to school, then go to work from ten a.m. to two p.m. and collect the kids after work, say Monday, Wednesday and Friday = 12 hours a week.

The national minimum wage as of April 1, 2023, is £ 10.42 an hour. 12 x 10.42p = £ 125.04p a week. And don't forget that this is the minimum wage. You may very well find a job that pays you more.

You all can appreciate that this amount of money coming in every week would make an enormous contribution and difference to your family's health and wellbeing, comfort and happiness. So you can get yourself down to the job centre and tell them exactly what you are looking for and the hours, etc. that suit you. So what are you waiting for?

Just do it tomorrow and wave the bad times goodbye.

Now let's say, for example, you are not on universal credit but you are just unemployed. The same thing applies to you; go and get that job; do not dilly dally any longer; get your arse down there, A.S.A.P. If you want money to spend, then there is no other solution. Remember there is no such thing as a free dinner; get out there, get a job – any job – just do it. And it will transform your lifestyle and situation overnight.

Again, tell the job centre what you want and what suits; bad situations require immediate action. Do not delay, make the move, good luck, and you will make progress.

When I came back home from abroad, I found a job in ten days. You don't have to be the sharpest knife in the kitchen to figure it out. It is just a necessary thing that you need and have to do.

From the beginning, when you start working, your status as a person improves, and so does your self-esteem. Your own confidence improves, and your own mental health and well-being increase. You eat better, you sleep better, you make new friends, you deserve and receive more respect. That feeling of being a second-class citizen disappears, and when that day finally arrives at the end of the month, when that day comes around and you know that your pay check finally drops into your bank account. The feeling of being independent and having now at long last getting your financial situation under control and having some money to spend. It will make you feel like a million dollars.

Do please remember don't go nuts with your first pay check; no doubt you will have debts, etc. to pay off; everybody does after being without work for a long period of time. However, please enjoy your hard-earned money because, well done, you have earned it and you deserve it.

Concentrate now on clearing your debts if you have any to pay back over the future months.

Contact anybody who you owe money to; make arrangements with these people to repay what you owe as quickly as you can, but don't overpay and overcommit yourself. Remember, you are in charge of your own finances, not the lenders.

Keep some in reserve and only pay back an agreed amount that you are comfortable with. Please remember the sooner you clear any debts out, then the sooner you will make real progress on your own road to recovery. Good luck, and God bless.

Let us now assume you have been in touch with the job centre and they are looking into your request to find work. Excellent because they will work hard to find you something and quickly. So stand by your beds and be ready to move fast if they get you an appointment for an interview.

Check your CV is correct and up to date; if not have it updated fast, you may need it quickly. Check your attire and clothes – what you want to wear on the day of your interview. Make sure it looks clean and laundered, and your shoes are clean and polished. You need this job, so give it your best shot. If you fail to secure it, then don't worry; there is plenty more out there to choose from.

OK. One day in the future, the telephone rings when you're least expecting it. The job centre is on the phone; they have organised an interview appointment with a nearby factory, and your appointment time is nine a.m. Next Monday morning with a lady named Mrs Smith. Wow, I told you that things move quickly.

Keep calm and, on no account, be late; try and walk in the door ten minutes early.

Attend looking calm and collected, not sweating and out of breath, so leave early.

Or better still get someone to take you there; get the lift of a friend.

Show her your updated CV. Answer the questions only when you're asked.

Try not to feel nervous; they want to give you the job; that's why you're there.

The normal procedure is they say, "We will let you know."

However, if you have got the job, more often than not, you will know before you leave.

Try your best to dress appropriately for the job in hand; this, of course, will depend upon your wardrobe. I know that it's difficult if you have not got much to wear.

Perhaps you could borrow some clothes from a friend.

Do not over or underdress; for example, if you're going for an office-type job, then wear a suit. And if you're a man, wear a tie.

Don't turn up in jeans and a tee shirt; if, on the other hand, you are going for a dustbin man's job, a refuse collector, or a street sweeper, then don't turn up in a tuxedo penguin suit and a bow tie. You get the idea and the picture. Dress code, get it right.

Once you have been offered a job, you're on your way at last; you'll be feeling great; it's been a long time coming. Go and have a drink if you want to celebrate.

Welcome back to the land of the living. It's been a rough ride and tough going, but you survived it and you got through it all, and you kept your dignity.

You all should feel proud of yourselves. Now you all can look forward again to a stable and prosperous and a normal and happy life for everyone. Well done, people.

No more eating humble pie, because remember, you can't keep a good man down.

Papillon.
Steve. McQueen.
Quote.
'Hey, you bastards, I'm still here.'

Chapter Nine
A Song Bird at Dawn

Hope is where the heart runs the deepest, when the darkest night turns into the sunniest day. Remember, the darkest hour is just before dawn.

Now wake every morning with new enthusiasm in your heart, grip this life by both hands, and make it work. Sometimes as a child, I would wake up occasionally in the early morning and lie in my bed listening to song birds singing in the new day.

A Robin, a Blackbird, and my two favourites, the Song Thrush and the cuckoo. These first three birds are cock birds.

Proclaiming their territory, telling other male birds that this is my patch, keep off.

The cuckoo calls cuckoo cuckoo to attract a mate.

It never ceases to amaze me, even to this day, how enthusiastic they are, how full of joy they are, and how full of hope they are even in bad weather and the rain. They fill me with inspiration and motivation to rise and face the challenges that the day will bring.

They are relentless in their efforts and pursuit of life; this mental attitude I've adopted myself many times over the years, and it has kept me alive through the bad times.

It also keeps you going through normal and good times. It puts a spring in your step.

So adopt this mental attitude yourselves from now on, and be relentless in your pursuit of life.

Some of you now should be out of the mire and the mud and on your way to a better future.

This new job you may have just started will be interesting and exciting, and you can't wait for your first pay check. Remember, don't go mad when it arrives; you have a long way to go before things get better. Although it's tempting, don't overspend. Control the urge to part with your hard-earned cash. Well, at least for the time being.

If you remember back into that dreadful winter last year when you didn't have two pennies to rub together, now things begin to improve, about time, thank goodness.

Just keep a tight rein on your finances, for the immediate future at least, so you can get back on your feet as quickly as possible. This should be your goal now, so slow down and take it easy. You have all your life and future ahead, and I'm sure you'll enjoy every minute of it.

Whatever and however the outcome develops, just keep in mind your immediate future needs and priorities. The main priority should be to clear all your debts as fast as possible before anything else. Of course this is entirely your decision, and you alone are responsible and in charge of your finances. This is the most sensible thing to do and the way to go, but we don't always act sensible do we.

Whichever and whatever route you choose with this new hope in your heart, you will find a new zeal and zest for your life that only a year ago you did not have.

What do you buy first when you need everything.? The answer is whatever you fancy.

You now can surge forward at full gallop without having any thought of bad times gone by in the past. Forget about everything; it's all water under the bridge and long gone. Focus your attention on the future, and you won't look back.

Whatever your age, you will have good intentions for tomorrow and beyond. Although when you are young, things do seem more important and exciting. When you're older, less so; however, you feel better, and that is what is important.

People years ago used to work all their lives up to pension age and, when retired, live a few years more and conveniently die around seventy years of age. Not so in this day and age people live longer; that is why the government keeps moving the goalposts forward. Their aim is to get pensionable age upward to seventy for all people, both male and female. Sold out by sticky-fingered politicians and their false promises once again.

Try and make sure you all begin to eat properly and healthily if you are not already doing so. Your mental health should be improving now, but if you think you're struggling, then have a talk with your doctor. All people are different; some just get on with their lives and others don't, so if you think you're one of these people, then get some help. Go and buy your nearest and dearest and the kids a treat if you can.

It doesn't have to be expensive; just don't go silly. On your days off, a day trip out to the seaside with snacks and treats on the way would be delightful. You all can do these things together now because you are earning money. What a fantastic improvement this is now from the way it was before. May it long continue. Keep up the good work.

We all need something to look forward to, even if it's only a small thing.

The kids can suffer enormously from deprivation and going without because they talk at school with other children who are receiving little treats from their parents, and they themselves are not receiving anything. Among ten thousand other things that need your attention, this should be on your priority list. I don't believe in mollycoddling children and wrapping them up in cotton wool, but there are limits.

I found that you can talk to them like sensible young adults from the age of about eight years upwards, explaining things to them in a calm manner, and they will understand perfectly. Tell them and encourage them that this situation will improve very soon. And that Mum and Dad are now or very soon will be working, and that means those little treats you are wanting are not too far away. Even young children need hope to make their little lives feel better; Mum and Dad need to give them encouragement; they need to feel wanted and cared for, and appreciated each and every day. With this kind of leadership and support, they will do well in school and at sports; they will eat better and sleep better; you are only young once. So I'm sure you will endeavour to do your best for them. After all, this is what parenting is all about, despite these difficult circumstances.

Chapter Ten
The End Game

The only reasons why we have endured these dreadful experiences and times. Of which we now wave goodbye to are the facts that money, like it or not.

Does rule our lives to a greater or lesser degree. It is a plain fact that we cannot function without it. The modest amounts we normally receive, the better our lives will become because every single thing we need, more often than not, costs money.

The car, the house, the holiday or vacation, food, drinks, clothing, etc.

The list goes on forever. This then brings to mind the absolute necessity to earn a living to the best of our abilities. Once experienced, poverty is not forgotten easily.

Remember the old saying, when poverty walks through the door, love flies out of the window. If you still have a partner, then well done. If you don't, then hard luck, but don't worry too much; try not to let it get you down. You will, in time, meet someone else.

If your partner deserted you in these circumstances and bad times, then good riddance to bad rubbish. Just remember you are not the first person this has happened to.

And you certainly won't be the last. Loyalties dissipate quickly when the money dries up.

So the importance of earning a steady and regular salary cannot be overstated or overemphasised. You all do not want those awful times to return ever again. I do hope and wish all of you the very best in the coming future. If you have got this far reading this book, then you all deserve it.

The children here deserve a special mention; they too have been through the same rough patch and endured all the hardships that came their way.

However, children are durable individuals, and they forget things quickly, but do keep a keen and close eye on them and their behaviour. It is possible that there could just be some underlying problem, hopefully not, but watch them anyway.

School attendance is another thing to consider and watch carefully. Statistics show recently, after the COVID pandemic, there are in excess of 125,000 children missing schools all over the country. It is a parental duty and responsibility to ensure that your own children attend school. The problem is sometimes they leave for school and they don't turn up. Or simply, they won't go. This then is a situation that has an underlying problem and needs to be addressed and looked into closely before it is resolved.

In my school years, no excuses were accepted by parents unless you were sick for absence from school.

No counselling was given. You simply received a clip around your ear and a kick up your backside. Things were a lot more simple back then. Things are very different today; however, if the problem persists with a child of your own, then there is help out there. The school teachers themselves can and do help the best way they can. The underlying problem could be bullying; it could be a new school; it could be because the child thinks its uniform is inferior to other children.

Many reasons can cause these problems, but whatever it is, it needs attention sooner rather than later, especially prolonged absence because the longer the child is off.

Then the harder it is to return them back to school.

As every parent knows, the cost of school uniforms can be a nightmare and a huge burden on families and their expenses. When you are short of money,

There is help from the government; go to WWW.Gov.U.K. School uniforms for information, or contact your local council; they may provide you with help.

School meals too are free for every child in reception up to year two. Also, if you're on benefits, there is help available for kids school lunches; make sure you ask them for information. No child should be hungry in school. Always try if possible to send them to school with some breakfast inside them. You cannot expect a child to learn and concentrate well in school if he or she is hungry. Child care is another matter for concern when parents have to go to work. If you have no choice but to pay privately, then you have my full sympathies. This situation can sometimes be uneconomically viable because the cost of the care costs more than you earn. Obviously another alternative needs to be found; this is where friends, family and grandparents come into play. Bless them all, because this is what family is all about. Footwear, shoes, etc. in the old days were always handed down from sibling to sibling. The shoes back then were more durable and made to last. Nowadays, however, they make them less durable on purpose, so they fall apart after a year or so, and you have to buy new ones. Also, the kids in these times would not wear their siblings shoes or cast-offs anyway because of the pride factor and the sheer embarrassment it would involve today.

If ever there was something to feel happy about, then now is that time. As things now get better, you can congratulate yourself on your achievements.

You have survived the most difficult times; you have coped on a very modest income and made ends meet. You have battled on and kept your tribe together in the midst of this difficult cost of living crisis. Very well done to all of you. This crisis will not disappear overnight; in my experience, once prices increase then they never return to normal and what they were previously. This means, in simple terms, that the prices we have now are sadly here to stay.

Housing also needs to be looked at here, as you may know anybody with their own home will automatically maintain the property and the upkeep of their home as it's in their own interest to do so. Even so, some grants may be available for insulation, double glazing, solar panels, heating, and so on. Check with your local council to find out exactly what is on offer and available. Try to take full advantage of any available grants to make your home as efficient and as comfortable as possible.

People who are renting properties are entitled to have their homes in good state of repair. This applies to renting properties from the local councils, or housing associations, and private landlords. If you experience any difficulties with repair work not being done and completed. There is nowadays legal advice you can take from professionals like disrepairlawyers.co.uk. Who will prosecute legally any council or landlords that refuse to comply with the law and maintain their property's in good state of repair. Do not pay good money every month for a property in poor condition.

Conclusion

So we have arrived at last in a better position and place than we were say one year ago. Thank the heavens; we are now in search of prosperity, and it's certainly a blessing and feels good. Hopefully now gone are those days of poverty, hunger, and want. The time, your time has eventually arrived, and your opportunity to make a stand.

I am convinced you will keep both feet firmly on the ground; you all will work hard and together to make these new times materialise into something special. And you deserve everything that will come your way. Never let it be said that working-class people are not worthy of a life that is more than just an existence.

I would like now to take the opportunity to wish each and every one of you my very best wishes for the future and the new year ahead.

> May prosperity continue and
> Follow you wherever you go.
> God bless and good luck.

www.ingramcontent.com/pod-product-compliance
Lightning Source LLC
Chambersburg PA
CBHW021638080526
44584CB00015BA/1521